Ten P
about V

ex libris

Candlestick Press

C000060739

Published by:
Candlestick Press,
Diversity House, 72 Nottingham Road, Arnold, Nottingham UK NG5 6LF
www.candlestickpress.co.uk

Design and typesetting by Craig Twigg

Printed by Ratcliff & Roper Print Group, Nottinghamshire, UK

Introduction and selection © Sasha Dugdale, 2019

Cover illustration © Hugh Ribbans, 2018
www.hughribbans.com

Candlestick Press monogram © Barbara Shaw, 2008

© Candlestick Press, 2019
Reprinted 2019, 2020

ISBN 978 1 907598 64 7

Acknowledgements:

The poems in this pamphlet are reprinted from the following books, all
by permission of the publishers listed unless stated otherwise. Every effort has
been made to trace the copyright holders of the poems published in this book.
The editor and publisher apologise if any material has been included without
permission or without the appropriate acknowledgement, and would be glad to be
told of anyone who has not been consulted. Thanks are due to all the copyright
holders cited below for their kind permission:

Matt Clegg, *The Sheffield Anthology: Poems from the City Imagined*, ed. Ann &
Peter Sansom et al (Smith/Doorstop, 2012) by kind permission of
the publisher. David Constantine *For The Love of It* (Smith/Doorstop, 2018) by
kind permission of the author and publisher. Sasha Dugdale, poem first published
in this pamphlet. Choman Hardi, *Life for Us* (Bloodaxe Books, 2004). Karen
McCarthy Woolf, *Seasonal Disturbances* (Carcanet Press, 2017). Stephanie
Norgate, poem first published in this pamphlet. MR Peacocke, *Finding the
Planes, New & Selected Poems* (Shoestring Press, 2015). Stephen Watts, *Republic
of Dogs/Republic of Birds* (Test Centre Publications, 2016). William Wordsworth
(1770-1850), out of copyright. Samantha Wynne-Rhydderch, *Ling di Long* (Rack
Press, 2018) by kind permission of the author.

All permissions cleared courtesy of Swift Permissions
(swiftpermissions@gmail.com).

Where poets are no longer living, their dates are given.

Introduction

Walking is a basic right, a basic task and a basic pleasure: crossing the ground by foot, measuring out the pace that is as much ours as a fingerprint, placing one foot on the ground and then the other, feeling every slight gradient as a mood swing, breathing and walking. Remaining at this most human speed – bi-ped, wheelchair, pram – the walking speed allows us to note the changing of leaf colour, a butterfly sunning itself, a piece of rubbish in the gutter, a newly painted door on a house. At this speed we see the seasons pass, buildings go up and rivers return to their source. Walks that repeatedly cover the same terrain give us that deep-rooted sense of place and belonging, and walks in new places remind us how the landscape changes imperceptibly and foreign and home are always interwoven.

I've walked all my life, and I've passionately undertaken that walking which takes us into hills and mountains and far away from other people – to places where all you can see for miles is silence or that man-made silence: a drystone wall creeping over the land. But walking is profoundly anti-elitist, anyone can strike out across a beach, a prom or a park, or along a stream or twitten. Anyone can fetch their day's groceries on foot or walk the dog, or nip out to the postbox. Anyone can join a protest walk or a charity walk and put their own individual pace in the service of others. There is nothing essentially better about one sort of walking or another, although there is (in my mind at least) a hierarchy of transport, with walking at the top and the car at the bottom!

The sense of walking as a pleasure should come to us tinged with the knowledge that for millions walking is still a mark of poverty and for millions more it is the exodus. Choman Hardi's poem here is a stark reminder that it is our privilege to think of walking in the mountains as a sport, rather than a last chance.

Sasha Dugdale

Lake

Sole self that day with a working pair of legs
A beating heart, attentive senses, climbed
High enough, far away enough, slowly
Against the river's hurry, quietly

Against the din of it, keeping close to it
And passing the highest shieling that an ash
Had burst as thinking will a head, I came
At dusk to a lake in its own terrain.

There the hills backed off in a spacious horse shoe
On that flat plane I was the only upright
The banks were low, looped in a contour line
The lake had nothing to mirror but the sky.

Sole self I bedded down close as I could
To listen: lapping, birdlife homing, settling
I watched the wind shunting the low black clouds
In tatters, fast, under a pale still ceiling.

Woke once or twice feeling a breath of rain
Glimpsed, silver on black, bits of a star-figure
Heard very high a flight of fellow humans
Touching on dawn after the black Atlantic.

David Constantine

Up on the Hill

A young Bulgarian who comes
to clear the old mattress and carpet
out of the bedroom
                         asks if Spring
always arrives so early here?
The forsythia's not out yet
so things must be as they should be.
                         There's an order
to the colours: snowdrop,
daffodil yellow, forget me not,
followed by brash sunset dahlia.
                         Up on the Hill
by the edge of Rush Common where
tree-fall debris mingles
with bottle tops, a pair of discarded socks
                         and crows
poke at the mud, the wrens
are nocturnal now, in order that
their song might be heard over
                         the babble of traffic
rumbling up the hill like a brook
inexplicably flowing backwards;
they sing, these birds
                         up above the smoke
you can only see from a distance, brown
and insistent as a river,
                         on nights
when we walk, lips purple
with wine, past the 24-hour shop,
arguing about who said what and
                         nothing that matters.

Karen McCarthy Woolf

Climbing Helvellyn

Ten years from now the path will look the same,
conceal the same old rocks lying in wait
for the newest *ingénues*. It's us who will have changed,
morphed from stags to men with mortgages,

yet unsure how, escaping from a feeling
we can't now name and couldn't gauge
the weight of the day we bounded up Helvellyn
camouflaged in tutus and pink antlers,

bantering at the glances of those heading back
to bills shouting from dressers, to sheds
that needed creosoting. Not for us, oh no, we had it all
in the bag: Vodka & Galaxy bars & all the blondes of England

to come. At the summit ten women on a chequered rug
staring at how far they'd travelled, had just begun
to pass round cling-filmed sandwiches as if they were
transparent presents and point little silver flasks

like wands at mountains still to climb
when we fizzed up with hello girls,
having a party? Kind of, they nodded,
we're a support group, we're *Widowed Under 40.*

Samantha Wynne-Rhydderch

Old Man Travelling
Animal Tranquility and Decay, a sketch

      The little hedge-row birds,
That peck along the road, regard him not.
He travels on, and in his face, his step,
His gait, is one expression; every limb,
His look and bending figure, all bespeak
A man who does not move with pain, but moves
With thought – He is insensibly subdued
To settled quiet: he is one by whom
All effort seems forgotten, one to whom
Long patience has such mild composure given,
That patience now doth seem a thing, of which
He hath no need. He is by nature led
To peace so perfect, that the young behold
With envy, what the old man hardly feels.
– I asked him whither he was bound, and what
The object of his journey; he replied
'Sir! I am going many miles to take
A last leave of my son, a mariner,
Who from a sea-fight has been brought to Falmouth,
And there is dying in an hospital.'

William Wordsworth (1770 – 1850)

walk in a wood after a long loneliness

you go into a wood, you find the place
where your father carved his childhood
there is the grain and the bole
the bark and the pen-knife's mark
he walked on but the tree remains, letters
widening with each year's ring

you search for clearings
where wind-flowers show white
and alexanders remember
their worldly journeyings
in bright green scatterings

you walk into a wood and stay there all night
you lie on leaf litter, hear
pheasants creaking beneath
a dark gloss of holly

you walk in a wood after a long loneliness

even now in the car, in the city,
you are in the wood, and the wood
is in you. remember? last night
you took my hand and

we were children, running up a bank,
grabbing onto a tangle of roots;
the tree above us leaned, sighed,
but it didn't fall

even when you walk the wood alone,
I'll find you by the stream below
the old carriage way, where late light
sends trees rippling into the water

Stephanie Norgate

24

To reach the place just ahead of you, what do you do?

The shortest way between two points – that straight line, the most straight of greatest renown. You put one foot in front of the other and carry on, repeating yourself. Until you reach the point ahead, assuming initial motion and no resistance.

You walk the straight line and you journey it.

No. Don't.

To read the place just ahead of you, set out backwards rising slowly and describe a circle complete but for the smallest measure between the place you left and the point you reach just ahead of it. And while you wheel right round towards yourself, measure a slow spiral if you like. That way you'll see everything about on the slow journey between two juxtaposed points. That way it is rich, most rich.

Think about it.

Topology of the word. Speech's own algebra.

Think on it.

Stephen Watts

Watchers

What do you think you're doing? my wife asks
Each time I bundle our kid in a sling
And take her out, early, before the trucks
Hammer the roads. We leave the estate, walk along
The dual carriageway for a mile or so
Then cross the central reservation. Once
We surprised a brace of rabbits where weeds grow
Behind a bill-board, but never again since.

We're heading for the spot where the road cuts
Over the river. We can wait a long time
And often go un-rewarded, but it's
Worth it for the off-chance of seeing him
Slow-step the ebb and flow with such grace.
My kid is going to know what a heron is.

Matt Clegg

Escape Journey, 1988

They force you to crawl, these mountains,
even if you are only 14.
Who made the first journey over them?
Whose feet created this track?

The exhausted mules carry us
along with the smuggled goods.
Sitting on their backs, climbing mountains
feels much safer than going down.
The steepness makes me lean backwards,
my back nearly touching the mule's,
then holding on becomes impossible
and I dismount.
It is easier, safer to walk sideways.

And from high up, I can see the white valley.
'A valley of plaster,' I tell my sister.
The mule owner says: 'It is snow.'
But I cannot imagine being rescued from this rough mountain
only to walk over the snow, covering the river.
I cannot imagine listening to the rushing water
passing by holes where the river exposes itself.

'You are too young to complain,'
the mule owner says,
and I look at my father, his little body,
and listen to his difficult breathing.
But then again, he's been here before.

Choman Hardi

The Old Roads

In memory of Dorothy Nimmo

Towards dusk or under light snow
the old roads reveal themselves
trodden into the hill
faltering at times in clay and gravel
gashed at a waterscour   picked up
as a strengthening scent   often their logic
cut by a counter logic
of intake walls   surefooted now
on a steady traverse   furrow
of descent   the cadence
abruptly lost

like the conversations
stitching our lives together
piecemeal so long   full
of inconsequences   laughs
digressions   forgetful pauses
abandonments   still in the old fashion
keeping in touch and always
working friendship deeper
that have come upon a stop
this jolt of severance
where no words find a footing

MR Peacocke

The Fall of The Rebel Angels

They didn't fall. It wasn't a pillar of legs and arms
a downpour of limbs, a shaft of flesh
like a rainstorm, dark over the sea –

No, they walked. They shouldered packs
laced boots, adjusted straps.
In hi-spec technical wear,
fleeces, gaiters, fearless, the angels
dropped from mountain top
and picked through the debris of rock
hopped over pavements, sundew, grikes
down scarps and slopes
entering the world on the thinnest paths,
the GRs from the stars
the trails, the aura
of a rope team on a glacier
the scramble, the clumsy jump
the odd angel on a bog,
jumping like a man from clump to clump
of cottongrass, falling into mud,
on a seraphic arse, over stiles and gates
and shifting slate in drystone walls,
built before the world knew how to fall,
and bathing in tarns, marvelling at
lambs, napping under pines
walking, walking in angelic lines.

And when they slept their up-till-then
unused legs kept walking in their sleep, their dreams were
of rights-of-way. And even when the coming of
day meant binding feet and the dampness of wings
still they hoisted their packs and took their flasks
and walked and walked, lacing the land
with endless small tracks, which led
(where angels did not fear to tread)
down into valleys and snaking over passes
shining tracks, visible to the naked
eye, the man in glasses, the woman
holding a map. Daily trespassing
angels, angels who walked, and fell
from grace into mountain streams
forgive us our lack
of dreams, we have forgotten
how to rebel.

Sasha Dugdale

Afterword

The cover illustration 'Head for the Hills' by Hugh Ribbans was created to mark the 50th anniversary of the designation of the Kent Downs as an Area of Outstanding Natural Beauty (AONB) and the 40th anniversary of the North Downs Way National Trail. The rolling chalk hills and deep valleys that characterise the Kentish countryside provide miles and miles of free open spaces for exploring. The North Downs Way is a designated National Trail that runs along the chalk ridge of the Kent Downs, providing over 100 miles of walking trails and wonderful panoramic scenery.

www.kentdowns.org.uk

www.nationaltrail.co.uk/north-downs-way